BASKETS

HarperCollins*Publishers*

BASKETS

Crafty ideas for beautiful baskets

Elizabeth Jane Lloyd

First published in 1997 by HarperCollins*Publishers* London

For HarperCollins
Editorial director Polly Powell
Project editor Carole McGlynn
Editorial assistant Becky Humphreys
Designer Paul Calver
Production Bridget Scanlon

Text written by Lucy Peel
All photography by Sue Atkinson

A CIP catalogue record for this book is available from the British Library

ISBN 0 00 412967/9

Colour origination by ColourScan, Singapore
Printed and bound in Italy by Rotolito Lombarda SpA, Milan

FOREWORD

I've always been afflicted with basket-mania, but it's an affliction that gives me enormous pleasure. I find baskets irresistible and over the years I've collected masses of them, all shapes and sizes, from intricately woven ones made by the Indians in Arizona, to the old, beautifully shapes strawberry baskets found in a market in the south of France. These have been added to my collection of sturdy, sensible baskets still made in the traditional way in England.

I can always find an excuse for acquiring a new basket and consequently they can be found in every room in my house, holding logs, needlepoint, make-up, kitchen stuff, shells, toys, papers on my desk, magazines, paints in my workroom – you name it, I'll find a basket for it. The reason for their appeal is that baskets are simple, pleasing objects: old or new, in their different styles, shapes and textures, they all have character. An ordinary plant in a plastic pot is turned into something quite special when the pot is hidden away in a rustic basket and cut flowers arranged in an old pudding basin concealed in a basket look a hundred times nicer than in a dreary vase.

So – it's no wonder that I leapt at the opportunity to write the Foreword to this book. In *Baskets* you will find imaginative ideas, beautifully presented and explained, encouraging you to look at baskets in a new light – even if, up until now, you thought of a basket just as something Red Riding Hood carried. These delightful ways of using baskets to make something special for yourself or for friends – whether you're filling the basket with gingerbread men or red roses – will turn you into a basket-case like me.

Nanette Newman

Contents

MAKING THE MOST OF BASKETS

Of all the items in common use by households across the globe, baskets must be among the most enduring. They provide an unbroken link which can be traced back as far as the times of such lost civilizations as the Ancient Greeks and the Romans. The flimsy remains of baskets have also been discovered in the tombs of Ancient Egyptians, and it is reasonable to assume that they were being used by our ancestors centuries before that.

Baskets were originally designed purely for everyday use, for such humble tasks as storing utensils or food, and for fetching and carrying. Their widely varying styles, which we find so attractive today, grew out of practical need, their shapes evolving according to the particular use they were going to be put to. Baskets for loaves, for example, needed to be long and shallow, while baskets for storing rice or cooking paraphernalia needed to be narrow and deep.

Over the centuries what were basically rather mundane household objects took on entirely different roles. People began to recognize them as objects of beauty in their own right and to realize their potential for many uses other than those for which they were originally intended. And so they were pressed into many other roles, from the everyday – such as storing newspapers – to the fun, as receptacles for pretty flower arrangements, for fir cones, dried grasses and seedheads, or even for Christmas baubles.

We are lucky today in that we have a veritable United Nations of baskets available to us, imported from all over the world. So while our own country's baskets may be both attractive and beautifully made, we can still satisfy our desire for the unusual: after all, it is always fun to try something different.

Baskets are constructed from natural materials, whether it be willow, rush, rattan or plywood. As we become more aware of our threatened environment, this becomes a definite plus. We are happy to use something entirely natural, especially if it means banishing non-biodegradable plastic containers to the rubbish heap of history.

Every household will have a basket or two somewhere, whether it be in day-to-day use or sitting forgotten in a corner. If yours are hidden away, now is the time to brush off the dust and turn your basket into something truly splendid, worthy of a prime position in your home, with the help and inspiration of the ideas contained in this book.

The glory of it is that it is so simple. There is no need to trek off to the shops and spend a lot of money on equipment: instead, whatever you have to hand can be pressed into use either to decorate or to fill your baskets. The key word is improvization. It is astonishing how something as plain and utilitarian as a shopping basket can be dressed up, with the help of a few ribbons or strands of ivy, to look unusual and special, worthy of being filled with something appealing.

Odd scraps of material can be pressed into use, to make a basic lining for an old basket, and suddenly you have a work basket to be proud of. The flower arranger's basic tool, oasis, is indispensable in a basket: with it you can easily create a wonderful centrepiece for a dining table or, if you are using a hanging basket, a flowering display to decorate a summer supper on the terrace.

Let the children get in on the act when creating brimming baskets: they will have hours of amusement decorating eggs for Easter, making fruit or figures out of bread dough, or cooking a multi-national collection of gingerbread people, all dressed in their national costume. A basket filled with such delights becomes a work of art in itself – and will be sure to make a children's party go with a swing.

Naturally, the time of year will dictate what materials are available to fill your decorative baskets, and the projects in this book are divided into different seasons. In the spring a wide variety of new bulbs appears, while summer brings a profusion of colourful blooms. In autumn, richly hued gourds, or golden-coloured dried seedheads and grasses, can take the place of flowers and look just as spectacular – as well as lasting a lot longer. Winter also provides a wealth of material to fill baskets, from Christmas candles, crackers or baubles to potted plants like poinsettias or early flowering, sweet-scented hyacinths or narcissi.

Some of the best fun can be had with *objets trouvés*, such as shells collected on a holiday at the seaside, or interesting feathers picked up on a walk through the woods. Everything can be put to good use.

There is nothing but the limits of your imagination to stop you making the best use of baskets. Hopefully, this book will give you inspiration and ideas enough to push those limits to their full extent.

SPRING

When the first daffodils raise their bright heads to the pale blue of an early spring sky, we know that winter is finally over. The spring season brings St Valentine's Day to look forward to, and Easter to prepare for. Easter is a particularly enjoyable festival, having none of the pressures of Christmas, yet just as many opportunities for fun.

Spring brings with it a host of cheerful bulbs, many of which will look wonderful in a basket. Simply pot them up in a shallow inner container, or line the basket with plastic first and plant the bulbs in it directly. This is a perfect way to bring a little bit of spring sunshine indoors: the bright colours of flowering bulbs will thoroughly dispel the gloom of winter.

SPRING PANSIES

Of all the so-called common flowers the little pansy must be one of the sweetest. With its jolly nodding head and open face, it is the optimist of the flower world. It is always cheerful looking and always bright – in colours as well as outlook.

This unassuming little plant is, nevertheless, one of the most popular among gardeners. And rightly so, for among its many varieties it is always possible to find one to bloom at a particular time of year. Pansies also come in every colour of the rainbow, which is extremely useful for anyone designing with flowers.

These numerous different shades and colour combinations illustrate perfectly how skilful nature is at contrasting as well as mixing and matching different colours and shades – such as deep rich purple and vivid yellow.

Wicker basket of pansies
Cheerful pansies and twining ivy have been planted in compost to create this brimming spring basket (*right*). The basket is lined with plastic first.

Putting on ivy and pressed flowers
Ivy is ideal for decorating a basket as it lasts a long time without water and has strong, flexible stems which can be threaded easily through the wide gaps in the basket work. Pansies, however, do not have this endurance, so dried, pressed pansies are the only option. If dried carefully (*see page 16*) they will keep their colour and shape, and their delicate papery-fine petals will provide an attractive contrast to the fresh living flowers. The pansies are wired to attach them to the basket.

WIRING THE DRIED PANSIES
1. Once the flower has been pressed and dried, take approximately 15cm (6in) of fine florist's wire and gently push it through the base of the flower head under the petals.
2. Fold the tip of the wire into a U shape with one end shorter than the other. Coil this short end around the stub of the stem and the rest of the wire.
3. Thread the wire through the sides of the basket and twist around the ivy stems to secure both.

All-year-round Valentine
For the truly romantic, love tokens need not be confined to Valentine's Day. All-year-round gifts with a love message are easy to make and always appreciated. A heart-shaped basket bursting with the bounty of the season is attractive as well as delicious.

Sprigs of bay leaves threaded through the wickerwork

Cherries attached to basket

Tasty soft fruits

Sculptural globe artichoke

Shallow basket in the shape of a heart

Tender new potatoes and peas

20

Petits fours

The name *petits fours* is French for little oven. However, some of these showy little delicacies are not baked at all and are more like confectionery than cakes.

Petits fours look wonderful made of marzipan, which can be moulded into all sorts of pretty shapes and unusual colours. Marzipan, also called *marchpane*, is an Arab recipe and was brought to Europe by the Moors. It is very malleable, so can be used almost like a modelling clay to be moulded/sculpted into a variety of shapes.

Marzipan

450g/1lb ground almonds
450g/1lb icing sugar
grated rind of a lemon
2 eggs, beaten
makes about 1kg/2lb

1. Mix the almonds, lemon rind and sugar.
2. Slowly add the eggs, stirring with a fork.
3. As the mixture becomes moist, mix by hand.
4. Once all the egg has been added, knead the mixture into a smooth paste.

To dye the marzipan, add a few drops of food colouring and knead well to coat evenly. To create an unusual frosted effect, sprinkle the coated petits fours with icing sugar (*see right*).

To make the roses above, mould small balls of marzipan into little petals. The tiny flowers decorating the hearts can be cut out with a metal stamp, available from most good cookshops.

GINGERBREAD

The warm, spicy taste of ginger combined with the crumbly biscuit pastry is a glorious taste sensation, equally suitable for an adult summer picnic or a children's party in winter. Gingerbread has a variety of associations. What child, or adult for that matter, does not know the story of Hansel and Gretel, the wicked witch and her gingerbread house, or the little gingerbread man running as fast, fast, fast as he can? Maybe because of all these fairy stories and folk tales, there is a tendency to associate gingerbread with Eastern Europe; however, ginger – one of the most versatile and widely used spices of all – is popular throughout the world.

Making gingerbread is fun, and so easy that it will keep children happy for a couple of hours on a wet afternoon – particularly as there is the prospect of a delicious treat once it is cooked.

The added advantage is that gingerbread actually improves by being kept for a couple of days, wrapped in foil or in a closed tin, before it is eaten, so it can be made in advance for any special event, such as a birthday party. A basket that is filled with home-made gingerbread makes a lovely gift. Try and choose an unusual basket – something slightly ethnic and rustic would be ideal – and 'dress' your gingerbread people in the appropriate national costume.

Gingerbread can be cut into any number of shapes, using ready-made pastry cutters. They can be used to make pretty decorations to hang from your Christmas tree, for example, or even to make love tokens, such as these two hearts (*above*). To attach a ribbon, simply push a small straw through your shape or figure before it is cooked: this will take out a small circle of dough, leaving a hole when the straw is removed through which you can thread your length of ribbon.

BASKET OF GINGERGBREAD
This trug-shaped basket is filled with an assorted 'family' of gingerbread people, their jolly faces and attractive costumes created with piped icing and coloured Smarties.

Tall-handled
wicker basket

Guinea fowl
feathers

Attaching feathers
Feathers add a dramatic finishing touch to a
basket of eggs, their fluffy softness contrasting
beautifully with the hard, smooth surface of the
eggs. They are easy to attach to the basket: just
thread the quill between the wicker strands and
secure with a fine piece of florist's wire.

Decorative
speckled
quail eggs

Soft downy
feathers

BLOWING EGGS

Before you dye or decorate your egg, you will
need to blow it. Have the egg at room temperature
– if it is too cold it will be hard to blow.

1. Take a large pin (a hatpin is ideal) and pierce
   both ends of the egg, making a small hole at the
   pointed end and a slightly larger one at the
   bottom.
2. Gently rotate the tip of a sharp pair of scissors
   in the larger hole to enlarge it to 5mm (¼ in).
3. With the pin, jiggle around inside the egg
   through the larger hole to pierce the membrane;
   this will enable the egg to be blown.
4. Hold the egg over a bowl and blow through
   the small hole, forcing the contents out of the
   larger hole.
5. Rinse the egg out, prop it up on paper and
   allow to dry.

DYEING EGGS

Commercial dyes are available in craft shops and
they are suitable for dyeing eggs. However, it is
fun to make your own natural dyes. Spinach
produces a lovely green, carrots an orangey-red,
and even coffee grounds can be used to create a
rich brown. But some of the best colours – from a
wonderful maroon to a reddish-brown – can be
obtained from onion skins.

1. Place skins in a saucepan of cold water and
   bring to the boil, then reduce the heat and
   leave to simmer for an hour.
2. Remove the dye from the heat and allow to
   cool before straining off the skins.
3. Place the eggs in the pan, ensuring they are
   filled with liquid dye to prevent them floating.
4. Return the pan to the stove and heat to boiling,
   before reducing to simmering point.
   Leave until the eggs are dyed to the required
   shade then rinse in cool water and allow to dry.

USING A FELT TIP PEN

Use a felt tip marker to create the look of folk-
type eggs by outlining a painted design or, as
here, drawing simple patterns on to a dyed egg.

1. Sketch the design on to a dyed egg with a pencil.
2. Draw over the pencil guide marks with your
   felt tip – the thickness of the line will
   determine the delicacy of your design.
3. Spray with a fixative to seal the pattern.

Intricately painted designs on dyed eggs

FERN-WRAPPED EGGS

You can use all sorts of natural materials to create beautiful designs. Small flat flowers, such as daisies, buttercups and violets, work well, as do small leaves. But for a truly delicate, elegant pattern a small frond of fern cannot be beaten.

1. Take a fine pair of tights and cut across the legs at intervals to make tubes.
2. Lay the fern face down flat against the egg and slide into one of the tubes, then gather the ends of the tube and pull taut so the fern is held firmly against the egg. Tie the ends firmly.
3. Dye following the method outlined on page 29, then carefully peel off the tube and the fern to reveal the design.
4. Spray on a fixative.

RESIST-AND-SCRATCH

Eastern Europeans use wax to create this effect in a method called Pysanka. However there is a simpler method of scratch carving called *sgraffito*.

1. Lightly sketch your design on to a dyed egg.
2. Using anything sharp-tipped – a nail, scalpel or tip of a very pointed pair of scissors – gently scratch away at the shell over your pencil marks until the undersurface shows through.
3. Spray with a polymer medium fixative – gloss or matt – for a professional-looking finish.

Three different ways of attaching ribbon

ATTACHING RIBBON

A pretty, brightly coloured ribbon is more than a means of simply suspending an egg. It will add a new dimension to any design. Here are a few simple methods of attaching a ribbon.

1. Tie or glue a thin ribbon to the centre of a short matchstick and slide the end of the matchstick into the largest hole in the egg. The stick will wedge itself crossways in the egg, holding the ribbon firmly.
2. Tie a knot in thin ribbon, then thread it through the eye of a long darning needle. Push the needle up through the egg, then unthread.
3. Fold a long length of narrow ribbon in half and tie the ends together. Take a piece of fine florists's wire and bend one end into a long U-shape. Push this through the top egg hole and out through the bottom one, then hook the looped end of the ribbon over it. Pull the wire back through the egg, taking the ribbon with it. Knot the ribbon at the top of the egg, either leaving the loop or snipping one end to leave a single strand. You may fold the ribbon back down over the egg to tie at the bottom.

Flower-wrapped design　　*Resist-and-scratch design*　　*Fern-wrapped design*

Easter-egg basket
The coiled raffia basket
is filled with a collection of
simply and elaborately decorated
eggs, showing the rich variety
of this folk art.

SUMMER

The profusion of flowers in the summer is overwhelming and quite glorious. Take advantage of the wonderful variety on offer to fill baskets and jugs for inside the house as well as outdoors. A beautiful arrangement cascading out of a hanging basket in the garden, or a spectacular display in a tall storage basket indoors, will make a dramatic focal point and convey the full glory of the summer season while being positively life-enhancing in its beauty.

FLOWER BASKETS

In summer we are spoiled for choice with the variety of blooms on offer. This is the time of year when the weather allows us to fling open all the windows and bring the garden into the house. Similarly, the abundance of blooms makes it so easy and tempting just to pick or buy a bunch of flowers and pop them in a vase without much thought. Of course they will look pretty, but it is so much more satisfying to go to a little extra effort and end up with something truly spectacular.

Baskets look particularly good brimming with flowers. Always take care when matching the basket to your flowers. Natural, meadow or woodland flowers look wonderful tumbling out of a rustic-style basket but would be lost in anything too formal, while more sophisticated blooms demand something really special. Try filling a basket with flowers to match the furnishings and colour in a room of the house, or even to suit a particular occasion or mood. Flowers have a language of their own, so an arrangement could carry an appropriate message. For example, the flower girl at a wedding could hold a basket of roses, symbolizing love, combined with something evergreen, representing life everlasting, or maybe honeysuckle, which stands for devotion. Children bearing baskets of flowers have in fact played an important role in festivals throughout Europe for centuries. The Corpus Christie and May Day processions, for example, would not have been complete without an entourage of little flower girls.

BASKET OF HOT COLOURS
Provided the basket is simple, an arrangement of cut flowers can be placed outdoors to provide a valuable focal point. The attractive fountain shape of the arrangement (*right*) was achieved with the help of florist's foam, which can hold stems in place even at these angles. The rich purple of the lizianthus combines with the bright colours of the asters and gerberas, set off by their halo of eucalyptus.

Everlasting flower basket
Silk, with its delicate texture and beautiful sheen, lends itself well to imitating the shapes and habits of different flowers. In fact a carefully chosen and arranged bouquet of silk blooms, as here, can be just as attractive as the real thing. This suspended wire basket, with its extravagant curlicues, is an excellent choice for such an opulent collection of artificial flowers. Sited near a window, it can be appreciated from both indoors and out and it will retain its beauty until you tire of the arrangement and wish to replace it with something else.

Candlelit basket
To light a summer evening's supper party in the garden, suspend above your table a hanging basket filled with moss and plants and surrounded by a quartet of candles (*left*). The combination of the flickering flames, the delicate trailing tendrils of foliage and the gently nodding heads of the flowers (in this case convolvulus) looks enchanting and will guarantee that your party is remembered as a magical occasion.

DISGUISING THE CHAINS
Hide the ugly chains used to suspend hanging baskets by winding ribbon or silky gift-wrapping tape around them (*right*).

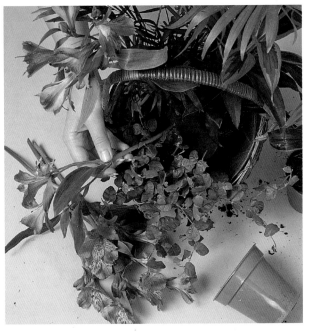

USING OASIS

Water-retaining florist's foam, known as oasis, has transformed the art of flower arranging. Prior to its appearance in the 1960s, a whole variety of materials, mainly wire, had to be used to hold flower stems in place.

Foam works particularly well when used with bushy plants or in conjunction with moss, which will hide both it and any ugly stalks. Before use, submerge the foam in water for about 20 minutes until it is soaked right through (weigh the foam down initially to stop it floating). Cut it to size using a craft knife or other sharp knife. Then simply push the stems of cut flowers into the oasis. Keep it topped up with water daily.

Try mixing cut and growing plants in a basket arrangement. For this basket, vividly coloured cut alstromeira lilies held in oasis have been combined with glossy green palms and other small indoor plants to create a sophisticated contemporary look.

POT-ET-FLEURS

The practice of combining cut flowers and growing plants in the same arrangement is called pot-et-fleurs. The joy of this method is that a permanent, evergreen framework can be transformed according to the choice of cut flowers added to it. It is also a clever way of spicing up any dull existing plantings.

Simply sink small, slim containers, such as yogurt pots, to hold the cut flowers into the compost around the growing plant, or arrange the flowers in oasis (as shown here), before filling the basket up with compost for the living plants.

Flower basket with bells
Combining hard and soft objects, such as these substantial bells and a collection of delicate-looking flowers can be extremely effective. The spiky thistles, in particular, make a wonderful contrast to the rounded smooth metal, while the gentle curves of the irises, the bright colours of the asters and the rough wickerwork of the basket add interest.

POPPIES

Wild flowers such as poppies, cornflowers, cowslips and grasses have been collected and arranged in informal bunches for centuries. Together with cornflowers and daisies, poppies were often seen as the weeds of traditional cornfields – yet it was these plants which were traditionally gathered to celebrate good harvests.

Poppies have several other associations too. The poppy motif, often entwined with ivy, appeared repeatedly in the Art Nouveau movement. This movement – with its organic lines and curling tendrils – was influential in persuading Europeans to re-evaluate their concept of beauty in plant terms.

At the end of the First World War the battlefields in France, where thousands of soldiers were horribly slaughtered, became smothered in scarlet poppies. And so the flowers which created these carpets of brilliant red became potent symbols of remembrance and consolation. Yet the poppy, with its peculiar, almost papery petals and sooty black centre, is above all a cheerful flower.

While fresh, living poppies are extremely beautiful, these flowers have the ability to delight even when dead. Dried poppy-heads are wonderfully sculptural and have many uses in dried flower arrangements. Shake out the tiny black seeds and save them to scatter on a bare patch of earth in the garden, then enjoy the amazingly rich pattern of bark-like textures the poppy-heads make when they are massed together.

BASKET OF SUMMER FRUITS
Arrange small bunches of dried poppy-heads informally around the rim of a basket and fill it with an assortment of ripe soft fruits. The rich red of the cherries and strawberries and the glossiness of their skins contrasts wonderfully here with the brittleness of the dried poppies, while recalling their glory when alive. If you can find some strawberries with foliage attached you will really have a spectacular offering with which to impress guests at the end of a lazy summer lunch.

Fresh and dried poppies

Never dismiss poppies as weeds.
They may grow wild in profusion,
but their good looks and brilliant
colours mean they can hold their
own against the most sophisticated
cut flowers. As they are relatively
short-lived, however, try drying
the seedheads for a
completely
different effect.

Poppy seedheads

Fresh poppies, with their delicate
papery petals, are transformed into
woody-looking seedheads when
dried. These are the pepperpots of
the plant world. Gathered into
small bunches, they are interesting
enough to be displayed on their
own, but for a really spectacular
effect bind them up with silky
ribbon or stand them in an
unusual basket.

*Freshly picked
poppies*

*Bunch of dried
poppy seedheads*

MAKING A POPPY SEEDHEAD WREATH

Simple to make, this looks delightful hanging in
the kitchen or above a fireplace. For an average
sized wreath you will need about 150 seedheads,
3m (10ft) of ribbon, and some fine florist's wire.

1. Cut the poppy stems to approximately the
   same length.
2. Gather the seedheads into small bunches (*see
   left*) and bind together with wire.
3. Arrange the seedheads so that they are evenly
   distributed along the bunch.
4. Bind the bunches together, using wire and
   ribbon simultaneously, to form a circle.

Poppy-head basket
Try wiring poppy-heads to the sides of an upright, wide-sided basket to transform it into something really special.

Wreath of dried poppy-heads

Sharp, wide-handled florist's scissors

Dried poppy-heads

Fine florist's wire

Poppies

Shaker basket of poppy-heads

The pure line and simplicity of the Shaker basket (*left*) dramatically offsets the richness and intricacy of the poppy-heads, while its lovely rich brown colour complements their lighter, subtle shades.

The Shaker influence

The Shakers are an American religious sect, whose members live in communities practising celibacy and praising God with vigorous dancing – hence their name. They make exquisitely simple objects – their tall ladderback chair being possibly the best known – as a form of living prayer or offering to God. These circular baskets, made in a series of diminishing sizes, are another example of Shaker craftsmanship: their beauty lies in their form and the unadorned use of richly coloured wood. Shaker designs are now very much in vogue.

Poppy eye, containing thousands of dark spores

Distinctive papery red petal

Weed-like stems

Small bud

The poppy symbol

In the language of flowers, red poppies stand for consolation, in part due to their association with the First World War.

DRYING AND USING POPPY-HEADS

Once you have collected your seedheads, gather them into small bunches and gently shake out the seeds over a sheet of paper. Hang the bunches upside down in an airy place to prevent the stalks drooping as they dry. The seeds can be scattered over a bare patch of earth for a splash of colour.

PICNIC BASKETS

Among most people's favourite recollections of childhood, there is sure to be a happy memory of a picnic. Just think of a hot, sunny summer's day and the joy of seeing the rug spread out covered with delicious goodies. Picnics are wonderful family outings, with great excitement for the children and surprises for the adults, but they can also be extremely romantic occasions.

While it is fun just to throw a few bits and pieces together and set off on the spur of the moment, it is also very enjoyable planning a picnic in advance and working out a theme of some kind – maybe one that fits the setting.

Themed picnics

Having a special theme works particularly well with children, who usually need something more than attractive scenery and good food to keep them happy for several hours. A few toys, some novelty food and the opportunity to make something which can then be saved as a keepsake, never goes amiss.

A picnic beside a river or lake is wonderful on a hot day, as even the proximity to water is somehow cooling, and there is always plenty to see and do by the water side, from observing small fish or skimming pebbles in the water from a riverbank to watching boats ply up and down on a lake or canal. So if you have a child's birthday, or another special occasion to celebrate, why not try a boating theme?

RIVERSIDE BIRTHDAY PICNIC

For a feast sure to delight children, take an old mushroom or fruit basket and fill it to bursting with egg or ham rolls, small sausages and tomatoes all stuck on to cocktail sticks, which in turn are stuck into an orange or a grapefruit. Don't forget the vital lemonade and lollipops, and to make it really special add balloons, toy boats to float and liquorice-allsorts necklaces (which the children could make for themselves after eating). No one could possibly be bored on this picnic.

Driftwood boats

These small boats (*left*) look beautiful above a child's bed and will be a constant reminder of happy summer days.

MAKING THE BOATS

Driftwood boats can easily be made from flotsam washed up on the shore or from odd pieces of wood. Paint the wood, stick on a twig mast, then attach eyelets through which you can thread string for rigging. Use scraps of fabric for sails.

Romantic picnic for two

Formal and impromptu picnics are fun, but mix in a little romance and they cannot fail to be a success (*left*). It is easy to make a delicious *al fresco* meal which will rival the smartest hamper. Simply pack an ordinary willow basket with edible treats and a bottle of wine or champagne, then add a red ribbon as a final flourish. Food always tastes delicious outdoors and a feast of olives (and olive bread), grilled baby poussins, French cheeses, delicious fresh fruit and chocolates will satisfy even the most jaded palate. For such a sumptuous spread only champagne will do, and a proper tablecloth to cover your picnic rug. To complete the splendid picture of elegance and romance, place a red rose in a vase in the centre of your feast.

THREADING LIQUORICE ALLSORTS

Liquorice allsorts are as colourful as the prettiest beads, and strung together they make jolly, as well as tasty, necklaces. Use a thick needle and cotton to thread the sweets, then tie the ends tightly.

SHELL BASKETS

Collecting shells need not be a hobby exclusive to children, in fact the gentle joys of beachcombing must make it one of the few pastimes guaranteed to appeal to young and old alike. Surprisingly it need not be confined to the summer, as a walk along a beach in winter, with the waves crashing dramatically on to the shore, can be just as enjoyable – and as productive – as an amble along the shoreline at low tide under a warming summer sun. It is also worth looking out for interestingly shaped pieces of driftwood and the sun-bleached skulls of seabirds.

While our seas may not yield the large, exotic shells found in the tropics, it can still provide a wonderful selection in many sizes and colours. In the eighteenth and nineteenth centuries, shells would have been displayed in collectors' cabinets, made into pictures or used to adorn frames and boxes. Today they are more likely to be arranged in a basket, where they form a fascinating collection of *objets trouvés*.

If you are not fortunate enough to have been to the seaside recently, or are short of shells, you could try visiting your local fishmonger or supermarket, as they would be happy to give you some scallop shells if they have them or to sell you a big bag of mussels. Mussels are relatively cheap as well as being delicious to eat. Their dark shells can look most attractive glued on to the frame of a bathroom mirror, and work equally well stuck on to a basket, the delicate blue colours of their insides creating a wonderful watery aura.

SHELL-DECORATED BASKET

Take an old basket whose shape you like – this one has a beautiful handle, whose twists echoes those of the shells – and decorate it with a selection of shells stuck on in changing patterns around the outside, the top and just inside the rim. Shell-decorated baskets can look equally good filled with a collection of exotic shells from around the world (as here) or with seasonal fruit or fresh flowers. This basket is the perfect embellishment for a shelf in the bathroom.

Shell Baskets

Starfish

Sun-bleached coral

Sea urchins create a decorative border

Driftwood comes in all manner of shapes

Skulls make interesting treasure

Irridescent blue insides of mussel shells

Mussel-shells basket
The flat sides of a mushroom basket make it easy to stick shells on to the outside.

A child's collection
This old mushroom basket (*above*), embellished with mussel shells and sea urchins, houses a child's beachcombing collection.

A pattern of snail shells
A collection of snail shells (*left*) arranged according to their beautiful markings makes a pleasing display.

STICKING ON SEASHELLS
Remove any sand and seaweed from the shells, then rinse and dry them. Place the shells on the floor to work out your pattern (rather as you would do when threading beads), then stick them on to the basket one at a time, using a strong instant adhesive bonding glue.

SCENTED LAVENDER

The word lavender comes from the Latin *lavare*, meaning 'to wash'. Besides using lavender oil as a massage oil to relax muscles before their games, the Romans and Greeks added lavender to their water before bathing. This was a wonderful idea as, apart from its lovely smell, it has a good astringent action, as well as the powerful calming properties found in its essential oil form. Its other medicinal uses are as an anti-depressant, and to combat tiredness and nervous headaches.

Lavender has also played an important role in domestic life through the centuries. Insects dislike its strong, sweet smell, so it was strewn among linen to ward off moths – with the bonus that it gave the laundry a wonderful fresh smell. In Tudor times, the washing was often spread out on low lavender hedges to dry, again imparting its fragrant smell to the laundry.

Lavender even has a culinary use. In Elizabethan times it was sprinkled on food, rather like salt and pepper, and made into a conserve. Even now more adventurous cooks experiment by adding some varieties (bar the French form, *Lavandula stoechas*, which is poisonous) to salad.

Colours among the many varieties of lavender (more than 25) range from rich blue-purple to delicate shades of pink and white. The flowers also come in different sizes, with the French lavender having the largest flowers.

While many people think of lavender as an essentially Mediterranean herb, conjuring up images of the vast lavender fields of Provence, it is also ubiquitous in English country gardens. It was probably brought to England by the Romans, and then its travels continued as it was taken to the New World by the Pilgrim Fathers on The Mayflower.

SUMMER PARTNERS
For a striking colour combination and a heavenly mixture of perfumes, combine blowsy English roses with a large bunch of freshly picked lavender and place them in a vibrantly coloured basket, anchored in a block of moistened oasis.

Lavender harvest

In this wonderfully fragrant summer's harvest (*left*), some lavender is gathered in bundles ready for drying (see p. 59) while the dried stalks await stripping for use in lavender bags. This rustic trug or 'truckle' is just the right shape of basket for laying out the long stems.

Lavender in the bag

Brightly striped material with rich purple ribbons make these pretty lavender bags a treat to look at, as well as to smell. Place one in a drawer to make your clothes or linen smell wonderfully fresh.

MAKING LAVENDER BAGS

Presentation is as important as perfume, so choose a decorative material for your bags and finish off with a bright ribbon.

1. Strip the dried flowers from a bundle of stems on to paper then transfer them to a sheet of fabric to conserve every atom of perfume.
2. Place in a warm, dry, airy place until they are thoroughly dry.
3. Sew up small cotton-fabric bags on three sides. Put in the dried lavender flowers and tie at the top with a ribbon.

Scented Lavender

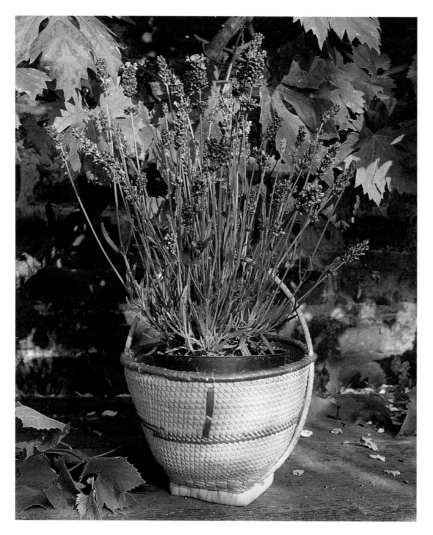

Drying lavender

For the best results pick your lavender early on in its season – that is, July – and early in the day, before the sun has had enough time to evaporate the volatile oils which give it its delicious fragrance. If any drops of dew remain, gently shake them off. Choose stems with petals that are just about to open.

The stems may be spread on a tray or flat sieve to dry, or else tied in small bunches and hung upside down (*right*) to prevent the heads from drooping. Allow them to dry slowly in an airy room.

Oil of lavender

Lavender stalks and flowers are crushed to extract its essential oil, often used in aromatherapy as a panacea for fatigue and stress-related problems.

GROWING A LAVENDER PLANT IN A POT

Lavender is a sun-loving shrub which will grow happily in a container. A small or medium-sized plastic pot can then easily be placed in a basket – such as this ethnic woven basket from Peru – for a moveable feast of fragrance.

Plant a young lavender in a pot filled with gritty, soil-based compost on top of a drainage layer of broken crocks. Water it regularly and feed occasionally. Trim off the dead flowers in early autumn and clip it over in spring to keep the plant compact. The lavender can be kept from year to year but will need repotting into a slightly bigger container in alternate years until it is mature.

COOK'S BASKET

As long ago as 3000BC flowers were being used to add colour and flavour to cooking. The Chinese first experimented with floral recipes, but they were soon followed in the West by the Ancient Greeks, then the Romans. Rose petals, either eaten raw, made into rose water or used simply as decoration, were a great favourite.

But while flowers were popular, herbs were absolutely indispensable. They provided perfume and colour, but above all they were valued for their flavourings and their medicinal qualities.

The Ancient Greeks discovered the healing power of herbs and the practice of herbal medicine then spread north through Europe. It was the Romans who brought herbs and knowledge of their use to Britain. However, with the Dark Ages, all this was lost, not to be revived until Norman times by monks travelling from monastery to monastery and taking their expertise with them. Crusaders returning from the Holy Lands, especially the hospitaller orders such as the Knights of the Cross of St John, also brought back and spread their knowledge about herbs and their uses.

In Tudor times herbs were plentiful enough to be strewn around houses to sweeten the atmosphere, as well as being considered essential in the kitchen. By the eighteenth century every plant and herb was pressed into culinary use – a somewhat risky practice, in fact, given the toxic qualities of some herb plants.

While we eat fewer herbs raw today, we enjoy their scents and flavours and appreciate their qualities as much. Just think of the bright yellow seedheads of fennel and the beautiful umbrella-shaped flowers of dill as well as leaves as diverse in shape and texture as those of bay, thyme and sage.

BASKET OF FLAVOURS

This basket, brimming with flavoured oils, fresh and dried produce and herbs, would delight any cook. Once the herbs are dried they last longer if kept in a dark, dry place, such as this tin container with all its different compartments.

Cook's Basket

Drying herbs
Herbs may be dried by being spread on newspaper or hung upside down in a dark, warm place immediately after harvesting. An airing cupboard is ideal. Turn them regularly and leave the door open to ensure plenty of ventilation.

Golden feverfew

Curly-leaved parsley

Common lemon balm

Sweet basil

Chives, from the onion family

One of the many varieties of mint

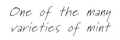

Dill leaves and flowers

Herb hanging basket
This old tiered vegetable rack (*left*) has been pressed into service of a different sort, for growing herbs. Hung by a French window, the herbs can be protected from too great a draught while enjoying the benefit of plenty of light.

PLANTING UP A HERB BASKET

Pack the baskets tightly with tarragon moss, which will form a firm base and hold the moisture in well. Line this with a circle of plastic or kitchen foil to prevent drips, then fill the basket with compost. Finally plant up your herbs, choosing a good selection for their looks and scents as well as their flavours. Water when the compost is dry and snip them regularly to enhance your cooking.

MAKING HERB OIL

Oil flavoured with your own fresh herbs is a real treat and makes a wonderful gift. The bottles will also look spectacular lined up on a shelf – they are too attractive to hide away in a cupboard.

1. Half fill a decorative bottle with sprigs of fresh herbs.
2. Fill up the bottle with olive oil – sunflower oil also works well.
3. Stopper the bottle and leave for a couple of weeks. For a stronger flavour, replace the herbs with fresh and leave for another two weeks.
4. Strain, leaving just a few sprigs in the bottle for decoration.

AUTUMN

As summer's long days gradually give way to autumn we can find pleasure in the glorious colours this season brings. The russets, golds and fiery reds of the changing leaves are spectacular, and the light takes on a special quality at this time of year, suffused with a beautiful golden hue.

This is harvest time, and as the crops are gathered in, we can all – city and country dweller alike – appreciate the bounty of the land and revel in the variety of its produce. The huge range of fruit and dried flowers, cereals and seedheads so plentiful at this time of year look marvellous, yet so natural, arranged in baskets. Such displays look as good in the bedroom as the drawing room and they are everlasting.

DOUGH BASKETS

One of the most readily available materials for modelling is salt dough, or sour dough. It is very cheap, being made from ingredients that can be found in most kitchens, wonderfully tactile and very simple to sculpt. It is also a truly international modelling material, since flour, water and salt are staple ingredients in most countries' cuisine.

Once kneaded and shaped, this extremely malleable dough can be fired in an ordinary oven, then painted with poster paints or watercolours. It lends itself to being cut into strips and made into a lattice-pattern base or 'basket' to hold small objects of any description. The finished dough products look very attractive varnished or, if you want to keep its beautiful golden brown colour, they can simply be glazed with egg white.

In Mexico this dough is known as 'bread glue', and the Mexicans make very intricate, delicate jewellery from it. It is also a key element in their Day of the Dead festivities, when it is made into numerous figures, the most popular being little skeletons, used to decorate the graves of family and friends.

Throughout Central and South America in fact, animals, scenes and characters from everyday life are immortalized in this humble dough. Ecuador has a particularly strong tradition with its ornate bread dolls, while in Peru they make little portable cribs for Christmas, with doors on leather hinges that allow them to open and shut.

ANIMALS OF THE ARK

This spectacular Noah's Ark looks complicated, but is not as difficult to make as it first appears. The boat has a simple lattice base, its sides, roof and ladder are just strands of dough, with a little extra decoration, while most of the animals are flat cutouts.

The reason this ark and its animal pairs look so professional is the careful and imaginative way they have been finished. The painting is detailed and the colours realistic, with attention paid to texture. A 'grain' has been scratched into the wood and a needle used to make indentations in the sides of the ladder, representing nails, and to define the animals' eyes, mouths and ears.

Dough Baskets

Salt Dough

900g (2lb/4 cups) plain flour
225g (8oz/1 cup) salt
450 ml (1 pint) water

1. Mix the flour and salt together, then add the water, stirring vigorously until the ingredients form a ball. This can be done in a food processor if you have one.
2. Knead until firm and pliable, with a smooth texture. Seal any dough not required immediately in a plastic bag to prevent it drying out.
3. Once you have modelled the dough into the desired shape(s), bake in a cool oven, between 275–325°F (135–160°C, Gas Mark 1–3), until hard and dry. Allow 30 minutes for every half a centimetre (¼ inch) of thickness. The hotter the oven temperature, the browner the baked dough.

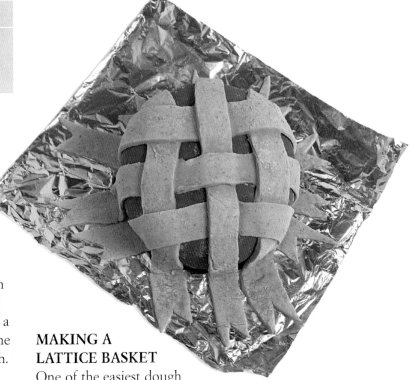

MAKING A LATTICE BASKET

One of the easiest dough baskets to make is the lattice basket. The trickiest part is the base, which needs to be gently rounded. However help is at hand in the form of an ordinary loaf, which is just the right shape to lay the dough over.

1. Roll the dough flat then cut it into six (or more) equal-length strips, trimming the ends into a V.
2. Place a loaf on tin foil, sprinkle with flour to prevent the dough sticking, then lay the strips over it in a lattice pattern.
3. Bake in a cool oven (see above) until hard, then carefully remove the bread.

Child's dough basket

Let children have fun making and painting dough baskets (*left*). Simply roll the dough into long snakes and plait it to make the base and handle. Paint with poster paints and fill with dough fruit.

AUTUMN HARVEST

Autumn is the time of year when we can sit back and take stock. We have enjoyed the summer, yet are ready for a change, and after all the weather isn't yet cold enough to be uncomfortable, or the skies grey enough to be depressing.

It is also a season for taking stock in a more literal sense. For the harvest is being gathered and food supplies laid in. Although those of us who live in towns or cities are far removed from this crop gathering, we can still share the satisfaction of this ritual and some of the traditions associated with it.

Making corn dolls is just such a tradition, and one common throughout the world, from America to India, with Poland and Eastern European countries sharing a particularly strong history of the craft.

Corn is one of the most basic ingredients of all countries' staple foods, whether it be ground to make rough, unleavened bread, the fluffiest French baguette, U.S. cornmeal or Italian polenta. So it is not surprising that the cultivation and harvest of corn figures strongly in many countries'

mythology. In fact, so important were the gods of grain that some pagan cultures even pacified them with human sacrifices.

It was a commonly held belief that the spirit of the corn would retreat as it was harvested, until eventually it was left stranded in the last remaining sheaf. Obviously the cutting of this last sheaf became the focus of various ceremonies and superstitions, and often the sheaf would be preserved, normally in some sort of decorative form. Hence the corn 'dolly' – a phrase which also covers numerous forms, from crosses and circles, to rattles and figures.

BASKET OF CORN DOLLIES
This handsome collection of corn dolls in a flat bread basket illustrates a good selection of different styles. There is a simple circle, made up from five-straw plaits, a lovely spiral rattle and, most complex of all, a wreath containing four hearts. The decorative bunches of wheat, oats and barley make an attractive, and particularly apt, backdrop.

Corn dolly angel

Realising the power of tradition, Christianity cleverly adopted some pagan customs as their own, as this corn-doll angel shows.

Basket of autumn fruits

'Season of mists and mellow fruitfulness ...' This sumptuous selection of rich-coloured fruit (*left*), with the succulent figs and ripe red plums beside the black grapes, would be perfect for an autumnal picnic.

Golden harvest

Cornflowers, poppies and daisies grow together with cereals in the wild, so it makes perfect sense to display such natural companions together in the home (*below*). The splash of brilliant red and blue brings to life this arrangement in a fruit picker's basket.

MAKING A CORN DOLLY BASKET

The five-straw plait is the basis of all corn dollies. The sides of this octagonal basket (*above*) are made of plain straws while the rim and the ribs, which hold it all together, are plaited.

1. For the sides, use the thickest section from the ear down to the bottom of the lowest leaf. Strip away any dead material, then soak the straws in cold water until they are flexible (about 15 minutes). Leave upright to drain.
2. Using natural-coloured thread, tie the thin ends of 5 straws around a narrow 40cm (16in) cane.
3. Bend the straws away from the cane at right angles to it, with two straws pointing north and one straw at each of the other compass points.
4. Bend one north straw over the west straw; bend the west straw over the south and so on.
5. Continue until the straws become too short, then slot the thin ends of five new straws into the plait. Continue until it is the right length.
6. Tie the end of the plait with thread, then leave it soaking in water until it is flexible enough to bend into a circle (about 10 minutes).

Thanksgiving

The American festival of Thanksgiving is a day set aside to celebrate the bravery of the Founding Fathers and to remember the hardships they endured. It is also a wonderful family occasion, an excuse for families scattered all over the country to gather together. This is especially important in America where, due to the number of different ethnic groups, it assumes more importance than Christmas, which is not celebrated as widely as it is in Europe.

As Thanksgiving falls on the fourth Thursday of November, it also doubles as an opportunity to give thanks for the harvest. This is traditionally the time of year when store cupboards should be groaning. It is the season of plenty before the exigencies of winter.

Autumn is drawing to a close, so most of the leaves are still on the trees, and the predominant colours are gentle reds and flaming golds. In New England, where the trees are at their most magnificent, makeshift stands laden with enormous, fantastically coloured squashes, often called gourds, line the roadsides. The flesh of many of these can be cooked – pumpkin pie being the best-known dish and the traditional dessert at Thanksgiving dinner – but some are used simply for decoration, or hollowed out to make lanterns for Hallowe'en celebrations.

Maize, another important crop in the US, was one of the earliest to be cultivated. Like the gourds, maize can be very colourful, ranging from bright yellow to shades of deep reddish-brown, and therefore makes a brilliant display in a Thanksgiving basket.

SEASON OF PLENTY

This typical American harvest looks quite at home in a Mediterranean basket. The long, tapering heads of maize contrast prettily with the full roundness of the gourds. This arrangement shows how vegetables can be just as attractive and decorative as flowers. When put beside flowers, such as these sunflowers and Chinese lanterns, the effect of the combined rich colours is quite spectacular.

Basket of maize
Even before the first settlers set foot on American soil, maize was being cultivated by some Native American tribes. After the harvest a few heads were always saved for decoration. The brown leather-covered handle and the red and yellow colouring of this basket blend well with the colours of the maize.

Dried oranges
This garden trug houses a seasonal collection of cut, dried oranges. The dark ivy leaves provide a good foil to the fruit. Twined prettily around the handle of the trug, they make it more suitable for use indoors.

Shallow sides are designed to hold cut flowers

Ivy leaves twined around handle

Cut slices of dried orange

Gardener's trug

Basket of gourds
Squashes come in an astonishing range of colours, patterns and shapes, from the flattish butternut squash to the better-known orange pumpkin.

CUTTING ORANGES FOR DRYING

1. Using a very sharp knife, cut about eight slim wedge-shaped indentations into the orange.

2. Peel away the wedge-shaped pieces of skin to reveal the darker flesh beneath.

3. Leave the orange to dry in a warm place such as an airing cupboard. As it dries, the orange will shrink slightly and the cuts will look more pronounced, contrasting with the flesh inside.

DRIED FLOWERS

During autumn and winter when there are fewer fresh flowers around, dried flowers and seedheads come into their own. They can brighten up awkward spaces and they look stunning mixed with fresh material. They can also effectively tone down rather too brightly coloured fresh flowers, rescuing a floral arrangement which might otherwise look too harsh. At the start of this century all design, floral included, underwent a revolution, with a move away from rigidity and formality towards a new minimalism. At this time Charles Rennie Mackintosh was using bowlfuls of coloured twigs for decoration, and seedheads – which would previously have been discarded – were kept to be used in simple arrangements.

Now it is accepted that nuts and vegetables, wheat, thistles and fir cones, as well as interestingly shaped twigs (tortured willow being very popular) can all be used to make beautiful creations. Even artificial flowers, long seen as the poor relation to fresh and dried, should not be dismissed out of hand. These have always been considered by some to be bad taste – possibly because the word artificial conjures up visions of garish plastic daffodils and chrysanthemums – but now, with the advent of delicate paper or fabric (often silk) flowers, they can be just as attractive as the real thing.

Always buy the best you can afford – the more expensive they are, the less likely they are to fade – and try and match the flowers to the season. There is something extremely disconcerting about seeing poinsettias in mid-summer.

EVERLASTING FLOWER BASKET

This elegant arrangement cleverly mixes dried flowers and seedheads with artificial material, yet it is virtually impossible to spot what is not real. The warm, muted colours seem to glow with the ghost of summer sun while still being the very essence of autumn. The sculptural-looking seedheads of poppies and thistles promise blooms to come, while the roses provide a permanent reminder of past joys.

Everlasting flowers

Everlasting flowers – statice, helipterums and helichrysums, also known as immortelles – have been prized through the centuries for their long-lasting qualities and the fact that they do not change much when dried. Without them there would have been no flowers at all indoors during the long dark winter months.

This garlanded basket (*left*) is a celebration of a bountiful harvest. The roundness and solidity of the fruit contrast with and highlight the papery delicacy and fragility of these everlasting flowers.

Miniature flower baskets

Miniature baskets can be arranged in groups of complementary or contrasting colours and also look appealing on their own. If kept out of the sun their colours will not fade and, as long as you blow any dust away occasionally, they will look this good all winter.

The seedheads of love-in-a-mist (*right*) have a striped appearance which looks charming when the heads are massed together.

The dried flowerheads of yarrow (*left*) form a lovely small yellow globe when displayed in a miniature basket.

THREADING DRIED FLOWERS

Everlasting flowers make a wonderful garland for a basket handle.

1. Sort out bunches of about six flowers and bind with tape or wire just below the flowerhead.

2. Working from left to right, lay your first bunch against the handle with the stems to the right, then bind the stems to the handle with fine florist's wire.

3. Place the next bunch so that the flowerheads conceal the stems of the previous bunch and repeat until the handle is almost covered.

4. Lay the final bunch the opposite way, so its stems hide under the previous flowerheads.

To attach the flowers to the sides of the basket, bind them in small bunches as before but leave long lengths of wire spare. Next cut the stems as short as possible and place the bunches against the sides of the basket. Feed the wires through the wicker and twist on the inside. You will find it easier to decorate the main body of the basket before the handles.

Mixed miniature posy

This is a posy for all seasons. The spiky eryngiums (thistles) look particularly striking and evoke a feeling of summer, while the dried poppy-heads look very autumnal. Other dried flowers used in this attractively coloured miniature basket include those with delicate-looking flowerheads, such as sea lavender, gypsophila, silvery honesty and straw or everlasting flowers. They are punctuated with slim, elongated grey-green eucalyptus leaves. The stems are anchored in a block of oasis cut to the shape of the basket (see p. 38).

Seedheads collection

The exuberant display (*right*) looks especially spectacular in this woven rattan basket. The combination of the Oriental basket and the wild profusion of seedheads, which are somehow the essence of autumn in the western hemisphere, is particularly irresistible.

The muted golds and browns of this collection gives it a glowing quality. Although the individual elements are humble, grouped together they look spectacular. The different textures and shapes – rough, spiky, fluffy and smooth – are endlessly fascinating, drawing the eye and giving this basket an enduring fascination.

Children will love playing at being squirrels and collecting seedheads such as these. It is worth taking a bag with you on walks in a woodland to carry any finds, while the more exotic seedheads can be bought at a good florist or garden centre.

Using silk flowers

Mixing artificial and dried flowers can produce excellent results (*left*). These silk roses are especially attractive, looking as full-blown and floppy as any variety of old English rose. Silk is the ideal material for making roses as its sheen matches perfectly the velvety quality of real rose petals.

Dried Flowers

Dried
seaweeds

Dried daisy-
like flowers

Spiky
artichokes

Poppyheads

Split
seedpods

Rattan
basket

WINTER

As the evenings shorten and we retreat inside, there are numerous consolations, not least the excitement leading up to Thanksgiving and then Christmas. Early winter is a time of planning and preparation and these two great family festivals offer the excuse to splash out, not just on food, but also on decorating the house.

A beautiful basket filled with gourds, fir cones or spiced oranges creates an atmosphere of opulence and occasion, and it is fun to bring as much as we can of the outdoors indoors, since we rarely venture out in this season. For most of us, the chance to gather around a blazing fire or groaning table is an infinitely more alluring prospect.

WORK
BASKETS

Baskets are the ideal receptacles for storing things. They come in so many different shapes that it is not hard to find one which suits your particular requirements, whether it be balls of wool or spools of silk. If you need to carry your work basket around, choose a basket with a deep handle, such as the shopping basket opposite. However, a shallower basket is more appropriate for trinkets or jewellery.

There is something immensely satisfying about a well-ordered work basket. Children will spend hours happily reordering reels of cotton according to colour, or sorting buttons into tidy piles and rolling up balls of elastic. For a work basket that is constantly on show, put in a little effort to ensure that it always looks presentable. Choose a pretty material for the lining and stitch compartments into it so that it looks tidy at all times.

Making a lining
This lining is made up of three sections. An oval-shaped piece of material forms the base, while two rectangular pieces make up the sides.

1. After cutting out and taking a turning all round the base, cut two pieces of fabric both the same length as the circumference of the basket, ensuring that one piece is as deep as the basket plus 5cm (2in) for turnings, while the other is about 2.5cm (1in) narrower.
2. Take a turning round the edge of both pieces, then lay them flat, placing the narrow length on top of the other. Sew the top piece to the bottom at regular intervals, to form the pockets, then sew the short edges together to form a circle.
3. Attach the wider piece of material to the rim of the basket with a loose stitch every so often.

SEWING BASKET
There is no risk of a muddle with this customized shopping basket designed to hold sewing equipment (*right*). The pockets in the lining keep each spool of cotton separate, leaving space in the centre for pin holder, needlecase, scissors, buttons and rolls of ribbon or tape. The tall handle makes it easy to carry.

**Knitting and tapestry
wools basket**
Balls or skeins of
wool and knitting
needles are awkward
to store since the
points of the needles
tend to make holes in bags,
while the wool gets tangled.
A shallow basket is the solution.
Everything is to hand, readily seen,
and it can be easily carried around.

Work bag

Make a bag-cum-basket (right) to keep silks and yarns separate and to hold any sewing work in progress. The drawstring will keep any fabric clean and it doubles as a handle.

Basket of beads

A shallow rattan basket with a compartmentalized fabric lining is perfect for storing beads, as they are easy to get at and easy to see. This is perfect if you make your own necklaces, earrings or other jewellery. The ethnic look of this rattan basket suits the chunky beads, while the soft fabric lining helps to prevent scratches.

Rattan basket

Native Indian beadwork

Fabric liner divided into 'pockets'

Home-made strings of ethnic beads

Loose beads for threading

Amber beads

African necklace

CHRISTMAS BASKETS

Even the most jaded adult will feel a flicker of excitement as Christmas approaches. For children, it is a time of glorious wonderment, almost unbearable excitement and glitter.

The traditional colours of Christmas – red, green, golden-yellow, orange and white – reflect the plants and the weather. The greens and reds are those of ivy and holly laden with berries, the white of snow and the delicate hellebores and early narcissi. Now, of course, the availability of more exotic blooms, such as poinsettias and forced hyacinths (with their heady perfumes, the strength of which is only matched by their vivid colours – blue, pink and white) have widened our choice.

We traditionally decorate our homes for Christmas using candles and crackers in these colours, besides natural materials such as fir cones and fruit. As well as colours and perfumes – nothing is as evocative as the smell of wood fires and the resiny scent of Christmas trees and pine cones – candles create a wonderfully Christmasy atmosphere. Their light is intimate, yet welcoming.

In many parts of Eastern Europe it is traditional to place a lit candle at a window on Christmas Eve as a sign of hospitality and to help travellers along their way – a custom said to hark back to the way the Christmas star guided the three wise men. Candlelight is elegant and extremely flattering at the same time, and the tall shapes of the candles combined with flowers, foliage, or even tree baubles, ribbons and bells, are very decorative. For a Christmas variation on the theme of pot-et-fleurs, combine a red candle with a potted hyacinth or fresh narcissi in a basket, perhaps for a visitor's bedroom.

SEASONAL MANTELPIECE

This unusual arrangement of small basket holders is North European in origin. The candles, berries, hips and ivy, along with the crackers and presents, give the mantelpiece a very festive appearance. It would be fun to light a candle for each member of the family and each guest, or even to represent each of the twelve days of Christmas by a candle.

Floating candles

A basket filled with floating candles (*left*) looks glorious on a table. The bobbing motion of the candles and their flickering light is mesmerizing, and mixed with the green of the ivy and the gold of the foil-covered chocolates will add a special touch of magic to a Christmas table.

Ivy threaded through the sides of a plastic-lined basket will disguise and soften its rim, as well as hiding the shallow glass bowl of water in which the candles float. A few dainty narcissi flowers floating alongside the candles and chocolates will release a heavenly scent.

Basket of crackers

Home-made crackers are much more fun than the bought variety and can be filled with gifts to suit each guest's tastes.

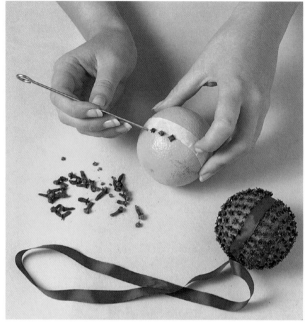

MAKING POMANDERS

1. Take a ripe, thin-skinned orange – preferably Seville – and bind it tightly with a circle of narrow sticky tape or a broad elastic band.
2. Using a skewer or fine knitting needle, pierce the skin and insert one clove at a time until the orange is covered. Follow the edges of the tape carefully to ensure the cloves are in neat lines.
3. Once the orange is covered with cloves, put it in a paper bag with a mixure of equal parts powdered orris root and cinnamon (ground nutmeg and allspice may also be added), allowing about a teaspoon of each per orange. Shake until it is completely covered.
4. Wrap the bag, orange and all, in tissue paper and leave in an airing cupboard for two or three weeks. Then peel off the tape before putting the pomander back in the bag for another couple of weeks.
5. Once it has dried out, decorate with ribbon, leaving a long length for a loop at the top.

The origin of pomanders

The word pomander comes from the French *pomme d'ambre* – meaning apple of amber; however, pomanders were originally perforated balls of china, silver or gold. These were filled with *pot-pourri*, dried herbs or spices, and in medieval times they were carried around by people to ward off infection. Orange pomanders – the cheaper, everyday version of these treasures – will perfume a room with their pungent aroma. Otherwise they can be placed in a wardrobe or in drawers, where their spicy fragrance will last even longer.

Pomander basket

This unusual star-shaped basket (*right*) is perfect for the Christmas season. The fragrant, spicily scented pomanders, with their glossy ribbons, are grouped together in a basket for maximum impact when they are not being hung on the Christmas tree.

DETAILED LIST
OF PROJECTS